All the words left unsaid…

Celeena Molina

BookLeaf
Publishing

India | USA | UK

Presentation by *BookLeaf Publishing*

Web: www.bookleafpub.com

E-mail: info@bookleafpub.com

ISBN: 978-93-5744-339-5

First edition 2022

DEDICATION

This book is to anyone in my life who believed in me and my writing. This one is the 1st of many. Thank you!

PREFACE

These are all the words I couldn't say...

Mind/Heart

Get out of my head
Get out of my heart
Just go
I don't want to love u anymore
I don't want to miss you
I don't want to think of u
Of us
Of what we could've been
All those empty promises
And fake dreams
Day dreaming of us being happy
N in love...
Love
Love
Love
I
Love
You
But I can't
I shouldn't
I don't want to anymore
It wasn't real
You didn't mean it
None of it was true
All your I love you's

Didn't mean a thing
You were a beautiful lie
A lie in disguise
Brought me to my demise
Until I realized
You're not the one for me
And you're nothing but a memory
A part of my history
A love that wasn't meant to be
But yet I still carry you with me
Through all my days
And even more at night
Repeating moments in my mind
Wishing I could turn back the time
And relive those memories
Of you and me...
You & me
You
&
Me
It sounded so good
If only you understood
What you meant to me
How your words pierced my heart
Right from the start
But you still couldn't see
All the things you put me through
The lies and deceit
Took my happiness from me

Because you changed overnight
With no warning in sight
You became someone different
Brought darkness into my light
Your words became less
Heartless and cold
You no longer wanted to invest
You started to fold
The Consistency faded
And you left me with nothing
But unanswered questions
And heartbreaking lessons
And yet I still miss you everyday
N These feelings just won't go away
And to God I have prayed
To no longer feel this way
Cuz I need to move on
Stop replaying the same sad love song
And finally be free
Because our story is clearly over
N u were never meant for me...

On Repeat

Your words are embedded in my mind
Wrecking havoc on my brain
Constantly on repeat
It's driving me insane

Something More

We didn't work out as planned
But after many sad nights
I'm finally beginning to understand

That maybe you didn't come into my life
& Maybe I didn't come into yours
That WE came into each other's lives
For a sole purpose of something more

It seems love wasn't the answer
Nor hate, that's for sure
& maybe not even for a lesson
But maybe for even something more

It's like we came from a different past time
One we once shared before
Maybe we were just best friends
& Never anything more.

Maybe we were in a band
And made amazing music together
With lyrics that connected us
A bond that would last forever

Maybe I was the clouds
And you were the rain
Or Maybe i was your joy
And you were my pain

Maybe you were the king of the jungle
And I was your pride
Where we stood tall and strong
Forever side by side

Maybe we were just kids
In the same grade school
Playing make believe
While breaking all the rules

Or maybe you were the darkness
And I was your light
Fighting for a chance
to finally shine bright

Maybe you were the moon
And I was the sun
Always crossing paths
But never truly becoming one

I Fucked Up

I fucked up
I know it
I feel it
Sabotaged the potential of something great
Something worth while
Something that could've been forever
Now it's just someone else added to the pile
I fucked up

I fucked up
I kept overthinking
Kept holding back
Kept finding a reason to doubt
There was something off track
I fucked up

I fucked up
I did something I shouldn't have
I did what I thought was right
I went with my intuition
Found out I was right
I fucked up

I fucked up
I turned something great
Into finding something wrong
Knowing the truth would hurt
But I knew all along
I fucked up

I fucked up
And it's what I always do
Keeping myself guarded
Til they have something to prove
Now I'm feeling broken hearted
And I don't know what to do
I fucked up

I fucked up
By seeking what I knew I'd find
What I hoped wouldn't be true
But couldn't beat my mind
So I did what i had to do
I fucked up

I fucked up
You fucked up
We fucked up

I fucked up
But so did you
We fucked up together
So now what do we do?

You

You're on my mind
More than just a little bit
I miss you when your gone
More than I'd like to admit

At first I thought it was just a crush
Just someone to pass the time
But it turned out to be way more than that
A new love that's now all mine

It's different from anything I've ever felt
Butterflies every time you're near
You make my heart literally melt
A feeling I no longer fear

I see a future with you
Something I didn't think could be real
I didn't know it was possible
To have someone feel what I feel

Never knew you would think I was beautiful
Didn't think you'd look past my flaws
Hard to believe you even want me
Never expected you to even call

But you've showed me consistency
Something I never had before
Continuously showing me love and attention
All these feelings I can't ignore

U make me feel loved
Without it being fake
I'm so looking forward to this new life with you
My heart is now yours to take

Overthink

I can't stop my mind
It's always on overdrive
Always thinking the worst
Imagining scenarios that never happened
Some wishing desperately that they would
Others I fear they just might

How do I choose?

I've loved you with every single nerve in my
body
All my atoms revolved around you
You were the one person who made sense
My dream come true
But Losing you was never supposed to happen
You were supposed to be the one
But life happened and things got bad
We were no longer having fun
Crying became a hobby
Sadness my everyday mood
I needed you to love me
The way I loved you
But u didn't when I needed you to
Only realized it when I was gone
So I tried to make sense of life
But then HE CAME ALONG
Showed me attention
Made me feel pretty
Acted like he cared
Didn't know I'd like the man in the city
He became a routine
Talking all the time
Realizing what we had in common
He was so kind

We started to catch feelings
And things got intense
Because the situation started changing
And it didn't make sense
But then He became distant
Started making me feel neglected
Barely calling or texting
Leaving me feeling rejected
But my feelings were still there
Didn't understand what went wrong
I always knew the situation was hard
I knew it all along
So I tried to do the same
and just let it be
But then a random text or call from him
Brought me back to reality
Thinking maybe he does care
& Maybe he likes me too
But he's still being distant
And i didn't know what to do
And you're still in the picture
Showing me so much love
Confusing my heart even more
I kept praying to God above
To help me figure out what to do
To lead me in the right direction
Even if that's away from both of you
My mind is in chaos
My heart torn in two

The man I love is walking away
The man in the city is too
So I'm left here feeling helpless
Lost and alone
Confused is an understatement
A feeling I've never known
I never knew this would happen
Loving someone and wanting another
You think it's an easy choice
Choose him or the other
But it really isn't that simple
Not for me anyways
Because after everything we've been through
U Left me scarred in so many ways
But I've been trying to look past that all
And see you for the man you are now
You look at me in a whole new light
Like I'm the perfect woman somehow
Telling me things I've always wanted to hear
& How perfect our lives could be
if I just choose you
I will eventually see
That we could be happy again
Even stronger in love than ever
That this could be real
We could actually be forever
And even though all that sounds great
It terrifies the hell out of me
Because in the back of my mind

Still lingers the man from the city
And what we could've been
If the circumstances were different
So the thought of what if
Has me feeling indifferent
Do I take the risk and just stay alone?
Do I go back to what I know?
Do I walk away from you both?
And see where my life goes?
Should I give up on everything?
And just start a new life?
Try to find happiness
With my babies by my side?
At this point I just don't know
Because the thought of losing everything
Has me losing all control
Like I can't get a grip on this
I honestly don't know what I'm doing
I wish I was stronger
Just get up and keep it moving.

Broken

Inside she's broken
Like shattered glass
But little by little she keeps trying to put herself
back together
Even when people keep taking bits and pieces
from her
Making her feel less & less and more unworthy
And yet she still keeps trying
Hoping that they won't continue to take from her
and leave her with nothing
Because eventually, she will no longer have
anything else to give...

Beautifully Broken

She's been through worse...
Felt the pain of loss so deeply, it consumed her
for years
She also knows heartbreak and what it feels like
to cry until she couldn't anymore
To reach out for someone who is no longer there
To being deceived and taken for granted
To being belittled and used
To yearn for what was once shared with another
To feel like she couldn't go on
But what she's currently feeling,
confusion, disbelief, and hoplessness
It's something unfathomable.
A feeling of angst from deep within
it's getting the best of her
& she just doesn't know where to go from here
Or what to do anymore
She feels lost and I don't know if she will ever
recover from this...

Forever Incomplete

19

She's been through hell and back
She's suffered so much
She's lost so much
She's forever incomplete
And through it all, she still keeps going
Never giving up hope that one day happiness
will finally find her
and embrace her with an unyeliding devotion
Promising to never leave

Waiting

She waits...
Waits for a call that will never happen
A text she will never receive
Or a knock on her door that she'll never get
She's drowning in words left unsaid
Feelings unspoken
Love unmade
A future that will never come to fruition
But yet she still waits
Believing that this can't be the end
Not before it even began...

Beautiful Mess

She saw her reflection
And couldn't recognize the person looking back
at her
The woman she saw looked broken
With a Tear streaked face
And A swollen pink pout
She just looked utterly defeated
& there was nothing in that moment that could
change how she looked or felt
because what she wanted the most
seemed unreachable and too far gone
If only she knew that this feeling wouldn't last
forever.
Because although She is beautifully broken,
She needs to believe that one day
someone will love her for all her broken parts
and for the amazing chaotic mess she truly is.

Open arms

When she loves
She loves with everything she has
She doesn't know how to let go
Even when everything tells her to walk away
Even when it's causing her pain
Even when there's no use in trying
She continues to love anyway
She may just be destined for heartbreak
But even then, she welcomes love with open
arms...

Not Enough

She's needy and likes attention
Not from just anyone
But from the one she loves
She doesn't always feel confident
So assurance is usually required for her
She likes to know & feel that the love is
reciprocated and not just one sided
She just needs to know that she truly is the only
one he wants on days when she feels like she's
not enough...

Empty Words

24

Words are never just words to her
She breaks them down
Tries to find the true reason behind them
Constantly repeats them in her mind
Fearing that those words are meaningless
But prays with all her heart that they're true

Rescue Me

Sometimes she just wants to be rescued.
Not from anyone or anything
But from herself

Warrior

She knows loss
She knows despair
She knows weakness
She knows suffering
She knows loneliness
She knows hopelessness
She knows abandonment
She knows heartbreak
But...SHE never gave up
For She is a warrior
who fights internal battles daily
& still finds the strength to look at the world and
smile

Music Love Language

27

She wanted to learn your music
Memorize your lyrics
Embrace your rhythm
And drown in your sound

She is Me

28

Don't let her self doubt and insecurities
push you away.
Because I promise you,
she hates feeling that way.
She wants to love herself,
even more than you do.
So believe me when I say this,
because She is ME too.

Music Heals

Listening to these lyrics
& I love that I can relate
It's like I'm fully invested
knowing how my heart will break

It's like I find these songs
That instantly bring tears to my eyes
It's the feeling of understanding
Their hurt and their cries

N We're never really alone
In how we truly feel
Because you can find the perfect song
Making what u feel actually real

Someone else has gone through this too
So it finally feels ok
To breakdown and have your moment
Because sometimes it's the only way

So I'll keep listening to these sad love songs
And continue to let myself feel
Because music is my solace
& this is how I heal…

"She"

She's fully aware that she's different
Too nice for her own good
Easily taken advantage of
Because her heart is pure
She believes in seeing the good in people
Even when they haven't been good to her
She believes in love, even though love has
broken her so many times before
She believes in happily ever after even tho
forever scares her
She believes in sacrificing her happiness to
make others happy
She believes in giving multiple chances even
when she only gets the one
She know she deserves the world, but the world
doesn't feel the same
She's just an easy target to be walked on
Easily fooled by those who know how to
She's just too damn good and yet she can't see it
She blames herself for things that aren't her fault
She doesn't know how to give up even when all
signs tell her too

She overly judge-mental of her self
She's her own worst critic
She has a million different laughs
She's cries at any given time
She start dancing at the most random times
She'll forever keep your secrets
She's a loner but also hates to be alone
She can be overly affectionate or not at all
She's beautiful and yet she can't see that
either…